Please remember that this is a library book,
and that it belongs only temporarily to each
person who uses it. Be considerate. Do
not write in this, or any, library book.

Great Americana

An Explanation
of the Map of Federal Lands

Manasseh Cutler

An Explanation
of the Map
of Federal Lands
by Manasseh Cutler

READEX MICROPRINT

Foreword

Long before the American Revolution, speculation in western land had excited colonial citizens. George Washington and many of his contemporaries were deeply concerned about investments in land beyond the Appalachians. As early as the 1740's, three or four companies, notably the Ohio Company, were organized to exploit land in the Ohio Valley. Several of the original thirteen colonies, including Virginia, Connecticut, New York, and Massachusetts, claimed trans-Appalachian lands, extending in some cases to the "Great South Sea." The question of the disposition of these claims vexed the new government of the United States and resulted in three famous Ordinances, those of 1784, 1785, and 1787, designed to settle the question of jurisdiction over the western country. In the meantime settlers had been pouring into trans-Appalachian territory, and speculation in land was rising like a fever. *An Explanation of the Map Which Delineates That Part of the Federal Lands Comprehended between Pennsylvania West Line, the Rivers Ohio and Sioto [Scioto], and Lake Erie, Confirmed to the United States by Sundry Tribes of Indians in the Treaties of 1784 and 1786, and Now Ready for Settlement*, published at Salem, Massachusetts, in 1787, is essentially a promotional tract to advertise the new opportunities in the Ohio Valley.

This tract was prefaced by a statement from Thomas Hutchins, a surveyor of the region, who had been named "Geographer of the United States," in which Hutchins testified to the accuracy of the information in the pamphlet. Hutchins himself was the author of *A Topographical Description of Virginia, Pennsylvania, Maryland, and North Carolina Comprehending the Rivers Ohio, Kenhawa, Sioto, Cherokee, Wabash, Illinois, Mississippi, etc. ...(1778)*.

During the 1780's the eastern states ceded to the United States their western lands, which the Congress of the Confederation then had to provide with some form of government. Thomas Jefferson was chairman of a committee that drafted the Ordinance of 1784, passed by Congress but never put into effect, which provided for the organization of sixteen states in the trans-montane region; some of these had fanciful names like Sylvania, Polypotamia, Pelisipia, Cherronesus, and Michigania. A second Land Ordinance of 1785 authorized the division of land in the West into townships six miles square with each township divided into sections of 640 acres. In each township, the Federal Government retained four sections; one additional section was designated for school purposes. Land would be sold for one dollar per acre with a minimum sale by the Government of 640 acres. The purchaser could subdivide his land and sell it as he saw fit.

Since most emigrants into the region would not have $640 with which to buy a whole section, land companies were organized to purchase blocks of land from the Federal Government and resell it on easy terms to emigrants. The most famous of these land companies was the Ohio Company of Associates, which obtained an authorization of Congress in 1787 to buy a million and a half acres on the Ohio and Muskingum rivers at the reduced price of less than nine cents an acre. This company was headed by General Rufus Putnam and the Reverend Manasseh Cutler.

In 1787 Congress passed the Northwest Ordinance providing for a temporary government of the whole region until it should have sufficient population to warrant the division into states.

The pamphlet reprinted here is an enticing description of the fertility and promise of the lands south of the Great Lakes. It carries the same appeal that earlier colonial tracts made to prospective emigrants in Europe. For a concise description of the land problem in the trans-Appalachian region, see Samuel E. Morison and Henry Commager, *The Growth of the American Republic* (New York, 1942), I, 259-263. A more comprehensive treatment is that by Thomas P. Abernethy, *Western Lands and the American Revolution* (New York, 1937).

A N

EXPLANATION

OF THE

M A P

WHICH DELINEATES THAT PART OF THE

Federal Lands,

Comprehended between Pennfylvania Weft Line, the Rivers Ohio
and Sioto, and Lake Erie ; confirmed to the UNITED STATES
by fundry Tribes of Indians, in the Treaties of 1784 and 1786,
and now ready for Settlement.

SALEM:

PRINTED BY DABNEY AND CUSHING,
MDCCLXXXVII.

NEW-YORK, 28th October, 1787.

HAVING attentively perufed the following pamphlet, defcribing part of the weftern territory of the United States, I DO CERTIFY, that the facts therein related, refpecting the fertility of the foil, productions, and general advantages of fettlement, &c. are judicious, juft and true, and correfpond with obfervations made by me during my refidence of upwards of ten years in that country.

THOMAS HUTCHINS,
Geographer of the United States.

EXPLANATION, &c.

THE great river Ohio is formed by the confluence of Monongahela and the Alleghany, in the State of Pennsylvania, about 290 miles west of the city of Philadelphia, and about 20 miles east of the western line of that State. In the common travelling road, the former distance is computed at 320 miles ; and, by the windings and oblique direction of the Ohio, the latter is reckoned about 42. These two sources of the Ohio are large navigable streams ; the former, flowing from the southeast, leaves but 30 miles portage from the navigable waters of the Potowmac, in Virginia; the latter opens a passage from the northeast, and rises not far from the head waters of the Susquehanna.

THE State of Pennsylvania have already adopted the plan of opening a navigation from the Alleghany river to the city of Philadelphia, through the Susquehanna and the Delaware. In this route there will be a portage of only 24 miles.

On the junction of these rivers, or at the head of the Ohio, stands Fort Pitt, which gives name to the town of Pittsburgh, a flourishing settlement in the vicinity of the fortress. From this place the Ohio takes a southwestern course of 1188 miles, including its various windings, and discharges itself into the Mississippi ; having passed a prodigious

length

length of delightful and fertile country, and received the tribute of a large number of navigable streams. The Muskingum, the Hockhocking, the Sioto, the Miami, and the Wabash, from the northwest; the Kenhawa, the Kentucky, the Buffaloe, the Shawanee, and the Cherokee, from the southeast, all navigable from 100 to 900 miles, discharge themselves into the Ohio; and yet the Ohio itself forms but an inconsiderable part of that vast variety of congregated streams which visit the ocean through the channel of the Mississippi.

THE Ohio, from Pennsylvania to the Mississippi, divides the State of Virginia from the federal lands, or the lands which do not fall within the limits of any particular State. These extend westward to the Mississippi, and northward to the boundary of the United States, excepting only the Connecticut reserve, which is a narrow strip of land, bordering on the south of Lake Erie, and stretching 120 miles west of the western limit of Pennsylvania. But a small proportion of these lands is as yet purchased of the natives, and to be disposed of by Congress. Beginning on the meridian line, which forms the western boundary of Pennsylvania, they have surveyed and laid off seven ranges of townships. As a north and south line strikes the Ohio in a very oblique direction, the termination of the seventh range falls upon that river 9 miles above the Muskingum, which is the first large river that falls into the Ohio. It forms this junction at 172 miles below Fort Pitt, including the windings of the Ohio, though in a direct line it is but 90 miles.

THE lands in which the Indian title is extinguished,

ed, and which are now purchafing under the United States, are bounded as before defcribed on the eaft, by the great Miami on the weft, by the Ohio on the fouth, and extend near to the head waters of the Mufkingum and Sioto on the north.

The Mufkingum is a gentle river, confined by banks fo high as to prevent its overflowing. It is 250 yards wide at its confluence with the Ohio, and navigable by large batteaux and barges to the *Three Legs* ; and, by fmall ones, to the lake at its head. From thence, by a portage of about one mile, a communication is opened to Lake Erie, through the Cayahoga, which is a ftream of great utility, navigable the whole length, without any obftruction from falls. From Lake Erie, the avenue is well known to the Hudfon in the State of New-York. The moft confiderable portage in this route is at the fall of Niagara, which interrupts the communication between the lakes Erie and Ontario. From the latter you pafs through the river Ofwego, the Oneyda lake, Wood's creek, and find a fhort portage into the Mohawk, and another occafioned by a fall near the confluence of the Mohawk and the Hudfon, at Albany.

The Hockhocking refembles the Mufkingum, though fomewhat inferior in fize. It is navigable for large boats about 70 miles, and for fmall ones much farther. On the banks of this very ufeful ftream are found inexhauftible quarries of free-ftone, large beds of iron ore, and fome rich mines of lead. Coal mines and falt fprings are frequent in the neighbourhood of this ftream, as they are in every part of the weftern territory. The falt that may

be

be obtained from thefe fprings will afford an in-exhauftible ftore of that neceffary article. Beds of white and blue clay, of an excellent quality, are likewife found here, fuitable for the manufacture of glafs, crockery and other earthen wares. Red bole and many other ufeful foffils have been ob-ferved on the branches of this river.

THE Sioto is a larger river than either of the preceding, and opens a more extenfive navigation. It is paffable for large barges for 200 miles, with a portage of only 4 miles to the Sandufky, a good navigable ftream that falls into the lake Erie. Through the Sandufky and Sioto lies the moft common pafs from Canada to the Ohio and Miffi-fippi; one of the moft extenfive and ufeful commu-nications that are to be found in any country. Prodigious extenfions of territory are here connected; and, from the rapidity with which the weftern parts of Canada, lake Erie and the Kentucky countries are fettling, we may anticipate an immenfe inter-courfe between them. The lands on the borders of thefe middle ftreams, from this circumftance alone, afide from their natural fertility, muft be rendered vaftly valuable. There is no doubt, but flour, corn, flax, hemp, &c. raifed for exportation in that great country between the lakes Huron and Ontario, will find an eafier outlet through lake Erie and thefe rivers, than in any other direction. The Ohio merchant can give a higher price than thofe of Quebec, for thefe commodities; as they may be tranfported from the former to Florida and the Weft-India iflands, with lefs expence, rifk and infurance, than from the latter; while the expence

from

from the place of growth to the Ohio will not be one fourth of what it would be to Quebec, and much lefs than even to the Oneyda lake. The ftream of Sioto is gentle, no where broken by falis: At fome places, in the fpring of the year, it overflows its banks, providing for large natural rice plantations. Salt fprings, coal mines, white and blue clay, and free-ftone, abound in the country adjoining this river.

THE undiftinguifhing terms of admiration, that are commonly ufed in fpeaking of the natural fertility of the country on the weftern waters of the United States, would render it difficult, without accurate attention in the furveys, to afcribe a preference to any particular part; or to give a juft defcription of the territory under confideration, without the hazard of being fufpected of exaggeration : But in *this* we have the united opinion of the Geographer, the Surveyors, and every traveller that has been intimately acquainted with the country, and marked every natural object with the moft fcrupulous exactnefs—That no part of the federal territory unites fo many advantages, in point of health, fertility, variety of production, and foreign intercourfe, as that tract which ftretches from the Mufkingum to the Sioto and the Great Miami rivers.

COL. GORDON, in his journal, fpeaking of a much larger range of country, in which this is included, and makes unqueftionably the fineft part, has the following obfervation:——" The country on the Ohio is every where pleafant, with large level fpots of rich land ; and remarkably healthy. One general remark of this nature will ferve for the

B whole

whole tract of the globe comprehended between the western skirts of the Alleghany mountains ; thence running southwesterly to the distance of 500 miles to the Ohio falls ; then crossing them northerly to the heads of the rivers that empty themselves into the Ohio; thence east along the ridge that separates the lakes and Ohio's streams, to French Creek— This country may, from a proper knowledge, be affirmed to be the most healthy, the most pleasant, the most commodious and most fertile spot of earth, known to the European people."

The lands that feed the various streams above-mentioned, which fall into the Ohio, are now more accurately known, and may be described with confidence and precision. They are interspersed with all the variety of soil which conduces to pleasant-ness of situation, and lays the foundation for the wealth of an agricultural and manufacturing people. Large level bottoms, or natural meadows, from 20 to 50 miles in circuit, are every where found bordering the rivers, and variegating the country in the interior parts. These afford as rich a soil as can be imagined, and may be reduced to proper cultivation with very little labour. It is said, that in many of these bottoms a man may clear an acre a day, fit for planting with Indian corn ; there being no under wood ; and the trees, growing very high and large, but not thick together, need nothing but girdling.

The prevailing growth of timber and the more useful trees are, maple or sugar tree—sycamore—black and white mulberry—black and white walnut—butternut—chesnut—white, black, Spanish and chesnut oaks—hickory—cherry—buckwood—ho-

ney

ney locuſt—elm—horſe cheſnut—cucumber tree—
lynn tree—gum tree—iron wood—aſh—aſpin—
ſaſſafras—crab apple tree—paupaw or cuſtard apple
—a variety of plumb trees—nine bark ſpice, and
leather wood buſhes.   General Parſons meaſured
a black walnut tree near the Muſkingum, whoſe
circumference, at 5 feet from the ground, was 22
feet.   A ſycamore, near the ſame place, meaſures
44 feet in circumference, at ſome diſtance from the
ground.   White and black oak, and cheſnut, with
moſt of the above-mentioned timbers, grow large
and plenty upon the high grounds. Both the high
and low lands produce vaſt quantities of natural
grapes of various kinds, of which the ſettlers uni-
verſally make a ſufficiency for their own con-
ſumption of rich red wine.   It is aſſerted in the
old ſettlement of St. Vincent's, where they have
had opportunity to try it, that age will render this
wine preferable to moſt of the European wines.
Cotton is the natural production of this country,
and grows in great perfection.

THE ſugar maple is a moſt valuable tree for an
inland country.   Any number of inhabitants may
be forever ſupplied with a ſufficiency of ſugar, by
preſerving a few trees for the uſe of each family.
A tree will yield about ten pounds of ſugar a
year, and the labour is very trifling: The ſap is
extracted in the months of February and March,
and granulated, by the ſimple operation of boil-
ing, to a ſugar equal in flavour and whiteneſs to
the beſt Muſcovado.

SPRINGS of excellent water abound in every
part of this territory ; and ſmall and large ſtreams,
for

for mills and other purposes, are actually interspersed, as if by art, that there be no deficiency in any of the conveniences of life.

VERY little waste land is to be found in any part of the tract of country comprehended in the map which accompanies this. There are no swamps; and though the hills are frequent, they are gentle and swelling, no where high nor incapable of tillage. They are of a deep, rich soil, covered with a heavy growth of timber, and well adapted to the production of wheat, rye, indigo, tobacco, &c.

THE communications between this country and the sea will be principally in the four following directions.

1. THE route through the Sioto and Muskingum to lake Erie, and so to the river Hudson; which has been already described.

2. THE passage up the Ohio and Monongahela, to the portage above-mentioned, which leads to the navigable waters of the Potowmac. This portage is 30 miles, and will probably be rendered much less by the execution of the plans now on foot for opening the navigation of those waters.

3. THE great Kenhawa, which falls into the Ohio from the Virginia shore, between the Hockhocking and the Sioto, opens an extensive navigation from the southeast, and leaves but 18 miles portage from the navigable waters of James river, in Virginia. This communication, for the country between Muskingum and Sioto, will probably be more used than any other, for the exportation of manufactures, and other light and valuable articles; and,

especially,

especially, for the importation of foreign commodities, which may be brought from the Chesapeak to the Ohio much cheaper than they are now carried from Philadelphia to Carlisle and the other thick settled back counties of Pennsylvania.

4. BUT the current down the Ohio and the Missisippi, for heavy articles that suit the Florida and West-India markets, such as corn, flour, beef, lumber, &c. will be more frequently loaded than any streams on earth. The distance from the Sioto to the Missisippi is 800 miles ; from thence to the sea is 900. This whole course is easily run in 15 days ; and the passage up those rivers is not so difficult as has usually been represented. It is found, by late experiments, that sails are used to great advantage against the current of the Ohio : And it is worthy of observation, that in all probability steam-boats will be found to do infinite service in all our extensive river navigation.

SUCH is the state of facts relative to the natural advantages of the territory described in the annexed map. As far as observations in passing the rivers, and the transitory remarks of travellers, will justify an pinion, the lands farther down, and in other parts of the unappropriated country, are not equal, in point of soil and other local advantages, to the tract which is here described. This, however, cannot be accurately determined, as the present situation of these countries will not admit of that minute inspection which has been bestowed on the one under consideration.

IT is a happy circumstance, that the *Ohio Company* are about to commence the settlement of this country

country in fo regular and judicious a manner. It will ferve as a wife model for the future fettlement of all the federal lands ; at the fame time that, by beginning fo near the weftern limit of Pennfylvania, it will be a continuation of the old fettlements, leaving no vacant lands expofed to be feized by fuch lawlefs banditti as ufually infeft the frontiers of countries diftant from the feat of government.

THE defign of Congrefs and of the fettlers is, that the fettlements fhall proceed regularly down the Ohio ; and northward to lake Erie. And it is probable that not many years will elapfe, before the whole country above Miami will be brought to that degree of cultivation, which will exhibit all its latent beauties, and juftify thofe defcriptions of travellers which have fo often made it the garden of the world, the feat of wealth, and the centre of a great empire.

To the philofopher and the politician, on view-ing this delightful part of the federal territory, under the profpect of an immediate and fyftematic fettlement, the following obfervations will naturally occur.

Firft. THE toils of agriculture will here be rewarded with a greater variety of valuable pro-ductions, than in any part of America. The ad-vantages of almoft every climate are here blended together ; every confiderable commodity, that is cultivated in any part of the United States, is here produced in the greateft plenty and perfection. The high and dry lands are of a deep, rich foil—pro-ducing, in abundance, *wheat, rye, Indian corn, buck wheat, oats, barley, flax, hemp, tobacco, indigo, filk,*

filk, wine and cotton. The tobacco is of a quality
fuperior to that of Virginia ; and the crops of
wheat are larger than in any other part of America.
The common growth of Indian corn is from 60
to 80 bufhels to the acre.* The low lands are
well fuited to the production of nearly all the above
articles, except wheat. Where the large bottoms
are interfperfed with fmall ftreams, they are well
adapted to the growth of rice ; which may be produced in any quantities. The borders of the large
ftreams do not generally admit of this crop, as
very few of them overflow their banks. But the
fcarcity of natural rice fwamps is amply compenfated
by the remarkable healthfulnefs of the whole
country ; it being entirely free from ftagnant
waters. It is found, in this country, that ftagnant
waters are by no means neceffary to the growth of
rice ; the common rich bottoms produce this crop
in as great perfection as the beft rice fwamps of the
fouthern States. Hops are the natural production
of this country ; as are peaches, plumbs, pears,
apples, melons, and almoft every fruit of the temperate zone.

No country is better ftocked with wild game of
every kind : Innumerable herds of deer, elk, buffaloe, and bear, are fheltered in the groves, and fed
in the extenfive bottoms that every where abound ;
an unqueftionable proof of the great fertility of
the

* GENERAL PARSONS, one of the Commiffioners of the treaty at
Miami, in 1786, has made in his journal the following note :—" Mr.
Dawfon has lived two fummers at this place—[*Little Beaver, near
Pennfylvania weft line*]—He fays, his corn is from 80 to 100 bufhels
per acre : Laft year, he planted 7 acres—plowed twice before plant-
ing, and hoed once only—and had 600 bufhels."

the foil: Turkies, geese, ducks, swans, teal, pheafants, partridges, &c. are, from obfervation, believed to be in greater plenty here, than the tame poultry are in any part of the old settlements in America.

THE rivers are well stored with fish of various kinds, and many of them of an excellent quality. They are generally large, though of different sizes: The cat-fish, which is the largest, and of a delicious flavour, weighs from 30 to 80 pounds.

PROVISIONS will, for many years, find a ready market on any of these rivers; as settlers are constantly coming in from all parts of the world, and must be supplied by purchase, for one year at least, with many articles.

Second. FROM its situation and productions, no country is so well calculated for the establishment of manufactures of various kinds. Provisions will be forever plenty and cheap. The raw materials for fabricating most of the articles of clothing and dress, are and will be the luxuriant production of this country. Though silk, cotton and flax are valuable in themselves, yet, by being wrought into the various articles of use and ornament, the expence of transportation is proportionably lessened. The United States, and, perhaps, other countries, will be supplied from these interior parts of America.

SHIPBUILDING will be a capital branch of business on the Ohio and its confluent streams. The Ohio, when at the lowest, admits of four fathom of water, from the mouth of the Muskingum to its confluence with the Mississippi, except at the rapids, which, at such times, interrupt the
navigation

navigation for about one mile. The defcent, in that diftance, is only 15 feet; and the channel, which is 250 yards wide, has, at no time, lefs than 5 feet of water. In frefhes, the water rifes 30 feet; and boats are not only rowed againft the ftream, but afcend the rapids by means of their fails only. It is the opinion of the Geographer, and others, who have viewed the fpot, that, by cutting a canal a little more than half a mile on the fouth fide of the river, which is low meadow ground, the rapids may be avoided, and the navigation made free at all feafons of the year. Hemp, timber and iron will be plenty and good; and the high frefhes, from February to April, and frequently in October and November, will bear a veffel of any burden over the rapids, in their prefent ftate, and out to fea.

THE following obfervations, by an Englifh engineer, who had explored the weftern country, were addreffed to the Earl of Hillfborough, in the year 1770, when Secretary of State for the North American department—at a time when we were Britifh colonies, and our country confidered only as the handmaid to Great Britain, in furnifhing raw materials for their manufactures.

"No part of North America will require lefs encouragement for the production of naval ftores and raw materials for manufactories in Europe; and for fupplying the Weft-India iflands with lumber, provifions, &c. than the country of the Ohio—and for the following reafons:

"1. THE lands are excellent—the climate, temperate; the native grapes, filk-worms, and mulberry trees, abound every where; hemp, hops and rye grow fpontaneoufly in the vallies & low lands; lead & iron ore are plenty in the hills; falt fprings are innumer-

C   able;

able ; and no foil is better adapted to the culture of tobacco, flax and cotton, than that of the Ohio.

" 2. THE country is well watered by several navigable rivers, communicating with each other ; by which, and a short land carriage, the produce of the lands of the Ohio can, even now, be sent cheaper to the seaport town of Alexandria, on the river Potowmac, where General Braddock's transports landed his troops, than any kind of merchandise is sent from Northampton to London.

" 3. THE river Ohio is, at *all seasons* of the year, navigable with large boats ; and, from the month of February to April, large ships may be built on the Ohio, and sent to sea, laden with hemp, iron, flax, silk, tobacco, cotton, potash, &c.

" 4. FLOUR, corn, beef, ship-plank, and other useful articles, can be sent down the stream of Ohio to West Florida, and from thence to the West India islands, much cheaper, and in better order, than from New York or Philadelphia to those islands.

" 5. HEMP, tobacco, iron, and such bulky articles, may be sent down the stream of Ohio to the sea, at least 50 per cent. cheaper than these articles were ever carried by a land carriage of only 60 miles in Pennsylvania, where waggonage is cheaper than in any other part of North-America.

" 6. THE expence of transporting European manufactures from the sea to the Ohio will not be so much as is now paid, and ever must be paid, to a great part of the counties of Pennsylvania, Virginia and Maryland. Whenever the farmers or merchants of Ohio shall properly understand the business of transportation, they will build schooners, sloops, &c. on the Ohio, suitable for the West India or European markets ; or, by having black walnut, cherry

tree

tree, oak, &c. properly fawed for foreign markets, and formed into rafts, in the manner that is now done by the fettlers near the upper parts of the Delaware, in Pennfylvania, and thereon ftow their hemp, iron, tobacco, &c. and proceed with them to New Orleans.

"It may not, perhaps, be amifs to obferve, that large quantities of flour are made in the weftern counties of Pennfylvania, and fent, by an expenfive land carriage, to the city of Philadelphia ; and from thence fhipped to South Carolina, and Eaft and Weft Florida—there being little or no wheat raifed in thefe provinces: The river Ohio feems kindly defigned, by nature, as the channel, through which the two Floridas may be fupplied with flour, not only for their own confumption, but alfo for carrying on an extenfive commerce with Jamaica, and the Spanifh fettlements in the Bay of Mexico. Millftones, in abundance, are to be obtained in the hills near the Ohio ; and the country is every where well watered with large and conftant fprings and ftreams for grift and other mills. The paffage from Philadelphia to Penfacola is feldom made in lefs than a month ; and 60 fhillings fterling per ton freight (confifting of 16 barrels) is ufually paid for flour, &c. thither. Boats, carrying 500 or 1000 barrels of flour, may go in about the fame time from Pittfburgh, as from Philadelphia, to Penfacola, and for half the above freight. The Ohio merchants could deliver flour, &c. there, in much better order than from Philadelphia, and without incurring the damage and delay of the fea, and charges of infurance, &c. as from thence to Penfacola. This is not mere fpeculation ; for it is a fact, that about the year 1746 there was a fcarcity of provifions at New Orleans ; and the French fettlements at the Illinois, fmall as they then were,

fent

sent thither, in one winter, upwards of eight hundred thousand weight of flour."

IF, instead of furnishing other nations with raw materials, companies of manufacturers from Europe could be introduced and established in this inviting situation, under the superintendence of men of property, it would occasion an immense addition of men and wealth to these new settlements, and serve as a beneficial example of economy to many parts of the United States.

Third. IN the late ordinance of Congress, for disposing of the western lands as far down as the river Sioto, the provision that is made for schools and the endowment of an university, looks with a most favourable aspect upon the settlement, and furnishes the presentiment, that, by a proper attention to the subject of education, under these advantages, the field of science may be greatly enlarged, and the acquisition of useful knowledge placed upon a more respectable footing here, than in any other part of the world. Besides the opportunity of opening a new and unexplored region for the range of natural history, botany and the medical science, there will be one advantage which no other part of the earth can boast, and which probably will never again occur—that, in order to begin *right*, there will be no *wrong* habits to combat, and no inveterate systems to overturn— there is no rubbish to remove, before you can lay the foundation. The first settlement will embosom many men of the most liberal minds—well versed in the world, in business and every useful science. Could the necessary apparatus be procured, and funds immediately established, for founding a university on a liberal plan, that professors might be active in their various researches and employments—even now, in the

infancy

infancy of the settlement, a proper use might be made of an advantage which will never be repeated.

MANY political benefits would immediately result to the United States from such an early institution in that part of the country. The people in the Kentucky and Illinois countries are rapidly increasing. Their distance from the old States will prevent their sending their children thither for instruction; from the want of which they are in danger of losing all their habits of government, and allegiance to the United States: But, on seeing examples of government, science, and regular industry, follow them into the neighbourhood of their own country, they would favour their children with these advantages, and revive the ideas of order, citizenship, and the useful sciences. This attention, from these neighbouring people, would increase the wealth and population of the new proposed settlement.

Fourth. IN the ordinance of Congress, for the government of the territory northwest of the Ohio, it is provided, that, after the said territory acquires a certain degree of population, it shall be divided into States. The eastern State, that is thus provided to be made, is bounded on the Great Miami on the west, and by the Pennsylvania line on the east. The centre of this State will fall between the Sioto and the Hockhocking. At the mouth of one of these rivers, will probably be the seat of government for this State: And, if we may indulge the sublime contemplation of beholding the whole territory of the United States settled by an enlightened people, and continued under one extended government—on the river Ohio, and not far from this spot, will be the seat of empire for the whole dominion. This is central to the whole; it will best accommodate every part; it is

the

the moſt pleaſant, and probably the moſt healthfuſ.

ALTHO' it is an object of importance, that Congreſs ſhould ſoon fix on a ſeat of government—yet,
in the preſent ſtate of the country, it is preſumed, it
will not be thought beſt that ſuch ſeat be conſidered
as immovably fixed. To take the range of the Alleghany mountains from north to ſouth, it is probable
20 years will not elapſe, before there will be more
people on the weſtern than on the eaſtern waters of
the United States The ſettlers ought even now to
have it in view, that government will forever accommodate them as much as their brethren on the
eaſt: This may be neceſſary, to prevent their forming
ſchemes of independence, ſeeking other connexions,
and providing for their ſeparate convenience. As it is
the moſt exalted and benevolent object of legiſlation
that ever was aimed at, to unite ſuch an amazingly
extenſive people, and make them happy, under one
juriſdiction, every act of Congreſs under the new con-
ſtitution, by looking forward to this object, will, we
truſt, inculcate and familiarize the idea. They will,
no doubt, at an early period, make a reſervation or
purchaſe of a ſuitable tract of land for a federal town,
that will be central to the whole ; and give ſome
public intimation of ſuch intention to transfer the
ſeat of government, on the occurrence of certain
events—ſuch as, comparative population, &c. This
would render ſuch transfer eaſily practicable, by pre-
venting the occaſion of uneaſineſs in the old States ;
while it would not appear to be the reſult of danger,
or the proſpect of revolt, in the new.

EXTRACTS

EXTRACTS

From the Letters of M. St. John de Crevecœur, Conful of France for the Middle States in America——lately publifhed in Europe.

"THE Ohio is the grand *Artery* of that part of America beyond the mountains ; it is the centre where all the waters meet, which on one fide run from the Alleghany mountains, and on the other come from the high land in the vicinity of the lakes Erie and Michigan.

"It has been calculated, that the region watered by thofe rivers, &c. comprifed between Pittfburgh and the Miffifippi, contains at leaft 260,000 fquare miles, equal to 166,920,000 acres. It is, without a doubt, the moft fertile country---the moft diverfified and beft watered foil, and that which offers to agriculture and commerce the moft abundant and eafy refources, of all thofe that the Europeans have heretofore difcovered and peopled.

"It was on the 10th of April, at eight o'clock in the morning, that we quitted the key of Pittsburgh, and gave ourfelves up to the current of the Ohio."

"This fweet and tranquil navigation appeared to me like an agreeable dream : Every moment prefented to me new perfpectives, which were inceffantly diverfified by the appearance of the iflands, points, and the windings of the river, without intermiffion---changed by this fingular mixture of fhores more or lefs woody ; whence the eye efcaped, from time to time, to obferve the great natural meadows which prefented themfelves, inceffantly, embellifhed by promontories of different heights, which for a moment feemed to hide, and then gradually unfolded to the eyes of the navigator, the bays and inlets, more or lefs extenfive, formed by the creeks and rivulets which fall into the Ohio. What majefty in the mouths of the great rivers which we paffed ! Their waters feemed to be as vaft and as profound as thofe of the river upon which we floated ! I never before felt myfelf fo much difpofed for meditation : My imagination involuntarily leaped into futurity ; the abfence of which was not afflicting, becaufe it appeared to me nigh——I faw thofe beautiful fhores ornamented with decent houfes, covered with harvefts and well cultivated fields ; on the hills expofed to the north, I faw orchards regularly laid out in fquares ; on the others, vineyard plats, plantations of mulberry trees, locuft, &c. I faw there, alfo, in the inferior lands, the cotton tree, and the fugar maple, the fap of which had become an object of commerce. I agree, however, that all thofe banks did not appear to me equally proper for culture ; but, as they will probably remain covered by their native forefts, it muft add to the beauty, to the variety, of this future fpectacle.——What an immenfe chain of plantations ! What a long fucceffion of activity, induftry, culture, and commerce, is here offered to the Americans !——I confider, then, the fettling of the lands, which are watered by this river, as one of the fineft conquefts that could ever be prefented to man ; it will be fo much the more glorious, as it will be legally acquired of the ancient proprietors, and will not exact a fingle drop of blood——It is deftined to become the fource of force, riches, and the future glory of the United States.

"Towards noon, on the third day, we anchored at the mouth of the Mufkingum, in two fathoms and an half of water. In order to give you

a weak

a weak idea of what I call the Anatomy of the Ohio, I will fpeak to you of this river, and let you have a glimpfe of what will one day be the utility of all its branches. It falls into the Ohio 172 miles from Pittsburgh, and is 120 fathoms wide; it is deep, and navigable for large veffels to 147 miles in the inner part of the lands; its current is moderate, and never overflows the banks, which are elevated, without being fteep; one of its branches approaches all at once the greateft of the fources of the Sioto, called the Seccaium, and the river Sandufky; this laft falls, as you know, into the great bay of the fame name, at the bottom of the lake Erie. It is towards one of the principal branches of the Mufkingum, that the great favage village of Tufcarawa is built; whence a carriage of two miles leads to the river Cayaboga, deep and rather rapid, the mouth of which, in lake Erie, forms an excellent harbour for fhips of 200 tons. This place feems to be defigned for a fpot for a town; and many perfons of my acquaintance have already thought of it. All the travellers and hunters have fpoken to me with admiration of the fertility of the plains and hills watered by the Mufkingum; alfo, of the excellent fountains, falt pits, coal mines (particularly that of Lamenchieola), of free-ftones, &c. that they find throughout.

" It was on the fourth morning, at day-break, we weighed anchor; and, in the fpace of three days of fweet and tranquil navigation, anchored before the Sioto, 218 miles from the Mufkingum, and 390 from Pittsburgh, in order to receive on board General Richard Butler, who came from finifhing fome negotiations with the Shawanefe: It is to him I am indebted for the following particulars of that fine river, upon the banks of which he had refided during five years of the war.

" The Sioto is almoft as large as the Ohio; its current is navigable, for veffels of a middle fize, to the village of Seccaium, 111 miles from its mouth. At this village commences the grand portage of Sandufky, which is but four miles----a communication much frequented by whites and favages, and confequently of the greateft importance. This river waters a champaign country, very luxuriant and extenfive.

" Those vaft lands, fo well known under the name of the plains of Sioto, begin fome miles above the river Kuskinkas, and continue almoft to Seccaium: They are watered by the pretty rivulets of Alaman, Deer, Kifpoko, &c. and by a great number of more confiderable ftreams: It is towards their fources, that you have a view of the fine villages of the Shawanefe nation. Many of them are from 25 to 30 miles in circumference; and, as if nature had been willing to render them ftill more ufeful to man, fhe has covered them with gentle rifings, upon which fhe has planted the fineft trees. Thefe plains are never overflowed, and their fertility is moft admirable. If a poor man, who has nothing but his arms to fupport him, fhould ask of me, where fhall I go to eftablifh myfelf in order to live more at my eafe, without the aid of oxen or horfes? I would fay to him, go upon the banks of fome rivulet on the plains of Sioto; there you will obtain permiffion of the favages of the neighbouring villages to *fcratch* the furface of the earth, and depofit your rye, your corn, your potatoes, your cabbages, your tobacco, &c. leave the reft to nature; and, during her operations, amufe yourfelf with fifhing and hunting."

" Every fpring a prodigious number of ftorks come to inhabit thefe plains; they are at leaft fix feet high; while feeding, they have their centinels to watch, and announce the approach of danger; fome time before their departure they affemble in large flocks, and upon a certain day, all together, raife themfelves flowly, and, by a kind of circular afcent, defcribe large fpiral paths in their flight.

" Finally, on the 10th day after our departure from Pittsburgh, we anchored before Louifville, having made 705 miles of navigation, in 212 hours and thirty minutes of time."